THE
*Archive Photographs*
SERIES

# HYDE

Hyde Chapel is situated in the village of Gee Cross. The first church built on this site was erected in 1708, the land being given by Joshua Thornley, the materials and labour provided by others. It was to serve Werneth, Hyde and Haughton. As the congregation increased they enlarged the structure in 1767. Due to the importance and prosperity caused by the growth of industries, especially cotton, it was decided in 1846 to erect a new church. The founders were Presbyterians who were unwilling dissenters from the National Church. They were cast out by the Act of Uniformity in 1662, and after that it was illegal to meet or worship in a public place.

THE
*Archive Photographs*
SERIES

# HYDE

Compiled by
Barbara Sole

**CHALFORD**

The Chalford Publishing Company
St Mary's Mill, Chalford,
Stroud, Gloucestershire, GL6 8NX

ISBN 0 7524 0335 4

Typesetting and origination by
The Chalford Publishing Company
Printed in Great Britain by
Redwood Books, Trowbridge

Young Andrew Sole jumps for joy! This view, looking over Hattersley from Werneth Low, was taken in the 1960s and shows some of the expansion that took place in Hyde at that time.

# Contents

# Acknowledgements

The author would like to thank the following people for their support and for permission to make use of their photographs:

Kathleen Adams, Mrs Ambrose, Mr Andrew, Mrs Ashworth, Beth Booth, W. Bowden, Cath Buckley, Mrs Burgess, Mrs Carter, Mr Copeland, Eileen Cooper, Mrs Crighton, Mr W. Cullen, Dorothy Hadfield, Mrs Harrop, Mrs Hilda Hibbert, Mrs Gillian Jackson, Mrs Kellet, Mr J. Key, Dorothy Lomas, Mr Marrow, Mrs Medhurst, Mr Middleton, Mr and Mrs J. Morris, Mrs Raven, Mr Neville Robinson, Mr Rowbotham, Mr Christopher Sleigh, Mr and Mrs A. Taylor, Mrs Taylor, Mrs Margaret Walker, Mrs Sandra Whittaker, Mrs Norma Wood, Stalybridge Library Archives, and the Documentary Photography Archives in Manchester.

The author would like to offer apologies to anyone who has not been included in these acknowledgements. I have relied entirely on contributors to provide the names of inviduals and also parts of the text. Apologies are also offered to anyone whose name has been spelt incorrectly, or who has been wrongly identified.

# Bibliography

Hibbert, Joseph, *A Lecture upon Hyde in the County of Cheshire and its Neighbourhood*
Higham, Fred, *Biographical Sketches and Pedigree of the Middleton Family*
Middleton, Thomas, *The Story of Hyde St George's Rowing Club*
Middleton, Thomas, *The History of Hyde and its Neighbourhood*
Nevell, Michael, *A History and Archaeology of Tameside, 1700-1930*
Various articles from old editions of the *North Cheshire Herald* and the *Hyde Reporter*

# Introduction

Hyde is situated seven and a half miles east of Manchester and five miles north east of Stockport. It is near the Peak Forest Canal, and the River Tame on the west divides it from the county of Lancashire. Hyde itself is in Cheshire. The villages of Gee Cross, Newton, and Godley, are now suburbs of Hyde. Since 1974 all have come under the Borough of Tameside along with Ashton, Dukinfield, Stalybridge, Audenshaw, Longendale, Droylsden, Mossley, and Mottram.

The area has been documented since AD 383, when it was known as Verneto ('alder woods'). The woods covered the Tame Valley and the area known as Hattersley. Over the years it was invaded by Romans, Vikings, Norsemen, and Danes. It is noted in the *Domesday Book* that 'The land was laid to waste due to plundering and raiding'. This period saw the introduction of manorial land settlement, and the woodland clearances began. In the fourteenth century Werneth Manor was established, and a dispersed settlement grew around the banks of the Low. Agriculture and domestic spinning and weaving were the main occupations until the factory system was introduced. Originally, Gee Cross dominated the cotton industry as it had a supply of springs and fast-flowing streams from Werneth Low. It was here that the first church, Hyde Chapel, was erected in 1708. Previously, worshippers had to cross the River Tame to Denton or walk to Stockport. At this time, Hyde consisted of a few scattered farms and a cluster of ten houses on Red Pump Street (now Market Street).

As a result of the Industrial Revolution, the quiet agricultural town of Hyde was transformed rapidly into a cotton industry area. Though water was still needed, coal became more important and Hyde had both. The population grew rapidly, and as people came into Hyde to work in the new factories homes had to be built and the necessary provisions brought in.

High production and industrial growth brought their own problems. Due to factory discipline and the long hours worked the family unit became less important than it had formerly been. Home became somewhere to sleep instead of a place where families worked together and helped each other. In 1812 there were wars in Europe and in America. Due to the lack of cotton from America, Hyde's trade diminished, and it was at this time that Hyde saw its share of Luddite unrest. Then, about twenty years later, came the Chartist movement, Hyde being one of the first towns to adopt the People's Charter. The cotton industry eventually became prosperous again, and the Chartist movement subsided.

One of the worst periods endured by Hyde followed the outbreak of the American Civil War. This inflicted a 'cotton panic' on the area. Hyde had become dependent upon the cotton industry and as it was suffering recurring crises in this area other trades developed and cushioned some of the depression suffered by the cotton trade.

The two raw materials found in Hyde were coal and clay. The clay was used for making fire clay ware, bricks, and mill chimneys. Coal had been mined in the area since the seventeenth century for domestic use, and later, as the industry developed, it became more important as it was used as a source of power. The development of technology and high production demanded more efficient transport than the pack horse.

The growth resulted in more pathways of communications. Between 1730 and 1830 turnpike roads were built, and the canals were constructed during the 1790s and 1800s. The railways were constructed between 1830 and 1880, all as a result of private speculation. Retail business and the distribution of foods and other goods also increased, and Hyde Market was established in 1851. Further growth in the local economy led to the development of service industries. Water supply, gas, and electricity, all at first privately owned, were later to be taken over by the local borough and Ashton.

The civic life of the town developed alongside economic and industrial growth. The townships of Godley, Newton, and Werneth were amalgamated in 1877 to form the Hyde Local Board, and the Town Hall was opened in 1885. The police station, fire station, hospital and clinic were opened in due course, and Hyde had become an urbanised area.

Factories also became specialized: there was engineering, paper-making, envelope-making, box-making, large rubber manufacturing works, calico printing, letterpress and lithographic printing, leather goods, glove making, book-binding, cabinet making, mineral water bottling, ice cream making, chamois leather making, brush-making, reed-making, and ribbon manufacture; and the list could go on.

Since the end of the Second World War Hyde has change its physical appearance. In 1954 there as a general clearance of unfit property. Old cottages vanished, and new, modern homes were built. The boundaries of the town extended, one of the most important influences being the building of the Hattersley Estate. This produced a substantial rise in the town's population, the first such rise in nearly one hundred years. The centre of the town has undergone two major changes since the 1960s. The latest – Hyde Renewal – is still continuing. In 1974, the M67 was built to ease the flow of traffic.

Some think that Hyde has changed for the better, but there are many who do not. Old Hydonians feel they have lost their individuality and that the people who made Hyde great in the past are forgotten. Those who look through this book may sigh for the old days, but it is not possible to bring them back. People have shared their memories with me, and I have enjoyed listening to them – especially as I was not born in the area. I hope that this collection of photographs will remind you of memories that had escaped you.

# *One*

# Rural Scenes

The first Hall was built during the reign of Elizabeth I; it was enlarged and refurbished in the 1660s. It was the seat of the Hydes family for over six hundred years. From the early Hydes sprang the eminent statesman Lord Chancellor Clarendon, and from him the mother of two of England's queens, Ann and Mary. The hall was pleasantly situated on low ground on the Cheshire side of the River Tame.

Apethorn Farm, Gee Cross. This farm dates from the fifteenth century, when it was a medieval long house. It is a cruck-framed building that was later, in the seventeenth century, encased in rubble and later in brick. The inside walls were filled with wattle and daub. On the night of 3 January 1831 Thomas Ashton, a mill owner's son, was murdered nearby. His assailants really meant to kill his brother. The reason for the crime was unrest at Apethorn Mill. In 1928 the lane was widened and the farmhouse was divided into cottages. During the summer of 1993 the building was fired, leaving just the cruck frame visible.

Haymaking, a popular activity with both children and adults. This particular haystack set on fire on Thursday 4 September 1913, and was still burning on the following Tuesday. Dove Farm was originally built in 1675 and was enlarged in 1781. It has been rumoured that the place was haunted by the sound of hounds.

Wood End Farm overlooking the valley of the Tame. The date over the door is 1632.

Joel Lane, Gee Cross, one of the main roads leading up to the top of Werneth Low. On the skyline you can see Hyde Chapel to the left and Queens Mill to the right.

Hare and Hounds in the 1920s. This was the oldest licensed premises in the district. Records show that there was an inn here in 1794. It was once a farmhouse situated on the old Roman road from Melandra, near Glossop, to Stockport. Between 1838 and 1850 horse racing was practised here. Walter Mansfield managed the inn from 1929 to 1983. When he took residence it was derelict: no water, electricity, or sanitation. Later, Walter installed his own generator. His motto was 'less talking, more drinking'. During the 1960's and 1970s, the hunt used to gather here on Boxing Day.

The Olive Tree Inn, Godley. This stood on Hattersley Road, where Wall's factory was.

Mottram Old Road viewed from Werneth Low before 1920. The road was built by a man named John Metcalfe. In his youth he lost his sight due to small pox, but this did not deter him from leading a full life. He went to 'see' London from his native town of Knaresborough, and he walked the 280 miles back to wed his lady love. Later he joined the army and fought in the battles of Falkirk and Culloden. He became known as Blind Jack. He built over 180 miles of roads, and many bridges.

Dowson Road, Gee Cross, looking towards Mottram in Longendale. It was named after the Reverend Henry Enfield Dowson, who was the minister at Hyde Chapel for 58 years. The building of the road commenced on 20 November 1923, providing employment for many. While it was being built Mr Dowson was able to sit in the rectory on Apethorn Lane and watch the work in progress.

Captain Clarke's Bridge. This bridge spans the Peak Forest Canal in Hyde and was originally named Wood End Canal Bridge. It is said that the bridge was built to divert the horse traffic to the other side of the canal in order that the Hyde Clarke family would not be troubled by the barges.

Mottram Old Road viewed from Gee Cross showing the old cottages dating from the 1800s, which are still with us today. It was in these homes that domestic industries such as spinning, weaving, and hat-making were carried out.

Bowlacre Lane, Gee Cross, 14 October 1913.

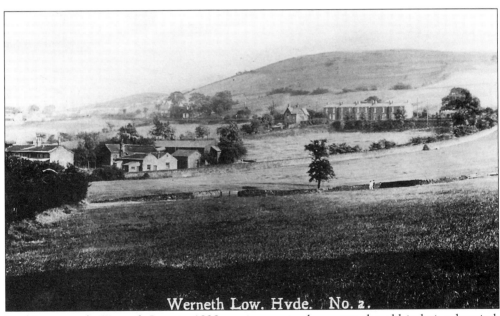

Looking towards Werneth Low in 1928 we can see in the centre the old isolation hospital, opened in April 1886. On that day the General Purpose Committee of the Hyde Council inspected the hospital. During that week some 600 to 700 people visited the hospital. During the First World War many Belgian refugees were housed here until homes were found for them.

Bears Wood, 1913, a favourite place for picnicking on summer days.

Brook Fold Wood, Godley. These woods are remnants of days gone by when the whole of the Tame valley was wooded, mostly with alder trees.

Bottoms Hall Wood. This is just off Mottram Old Road, leading towards the River Etherow. In 1461 a hall was built, which was refurbished in 1690. Bottoms Hall still stands today.

The foot road to Windy Harbour, on Werneth Low, in 1910. This was a favourite walking place, then and now. The Low is at the foot of the Pennines and from the top one may see Manchester, Oldham, Rochdale, Marple, Stockport, and Winter Hill. On a very clear day the Welsh hills are just visible. The summit of the hill was purchased by the people of Hyde to build a war memorial in honour of those who fell during the First World War.

Ash Cottage on the Low, with Hyde Chapel to the right. Here, at one time, the owner ran a small hatting business.

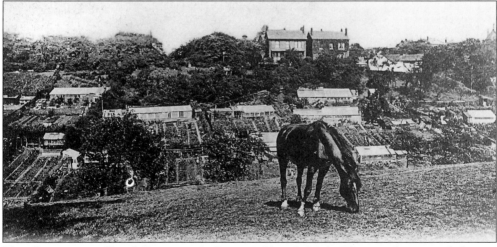

The allotments on Church Brow near St George's Church, Hyde. These gardens provided many a family with much-needed fresh produce during hard times. Many of the gardeners lived in terraced houses that had little or no garden space.

The stocks at Gee Cross. At one time the stocks were outside Hyde Chapel's churchyard. It was only when a small row of cottages was demolished in 1888 that the boundary of the church ground was extended. On one of the posts is engraved 'H.B. G.C. 1912'. H.B. could possibly be the initials of the person who erected them and this was possibly a member of the Booth family, who owned large acres of land around the area. G.C. stands for Gee Cross.

Mottram Old Road.

Sawyer Brow, which stretched from Victoria Street, Newton, to Hall Bottom Valley leading to the old highway known as Muslin Street. In 1829, people who were found guilty of crimes other than murder still often faced the death penalty. In that year John Woodhouse was hanged in Chester for the rape of his daughter. His relatives brought his body back home to Sawyer Brow and exhibited it to the locals for a small charge. Eventually the family left the house and from then on it was reported to be haunted. People said that they had seen John's ghost with the hangman's rope around his neck.

# Two
# Homes and Buildings of Hyde

Mill Lane, with Kingston Mill chimney in the background.

The Lumn, Hyde, in the course of demolition on 22 August 1913. The farm used to stand opposite St Thomas's Church on Lumn Road in the area now covered by Orchard Street and Tom Shepley Street. It was built in 1509 and over the years had little alteration. In 1612 one Richard Shepley purchased the estate, and it remained in that family for 244 years.

Another medieval cruck-framed structure was Newton Hall. In Roman times there was a track that ran up the hill from the River Tame, just below the Hall, all the way to Melandra Castle near Glossop, which is about three miles to the east. This photograph shows the Hall in 1900. In 1968, the Hall was going to be demolished and Sir George Kenyon had the hall restored in 1970.

During the sixteenth century, when there was little industry in Hyde, some refugees came over from Holland and started a glass-blowing factory near Hyde Hall. They settled in this cottage, later named Glass House Fold. Remnants of glass have been found in the area and they can be seen in Pilkingtons Glass Museum.

Cottages in the hollow at Kingston, showing the old road to the ford across the Tame.

Nimble Nook at Hattersley, where the junction of Stockport Road and Underwood Road is.

The Old Rising Sun at Hattersley.

Highham Farm on Werneth Low in its heyday. For many years it was uninhabited and it fell derelict. Now it has been converted into a country park offering conducted tours of the area, and the wardens also look after the land on the summit of the Low, which was purchased by the people of Hyde in memory of the men who died during the First World War.

Gower Hey Woods in Gee Cross was once a carefully kept woodland where families lived and couples strolled. Around the cottages there was a thriving market garden which has long since disappeared under a tangle of undergrowth. Miss Jessie Baddeley of Newton's family lived there for more than two generations. She recalls that children used to pitch tents there in the glade behind the cottages. The big houses that still border the woods were inhabited by local gentry, among them Thomas Middleton, the author of many books on Hyde.

At the top of Joel Lane in Gee Cross we have Werneth Low Road. The house on the left became a post office and general store. The centre house served refreshments to the passers-by.

Ralph Fold in Gee Cross was built like many other folds, to protect family, workers, and stock after the end of the wars which took place during George III's reign. Soldiers from the returning armies had no jobs and were forced to scavenge for their living. Houses built close together, forming a community, offered some protection. In 1785 it was owned by William Brocklehurst. These farmers supplemented their income by cloth production, fustian, and linen handloom weaving. A Gee Cross man, Walter Stopford, helped demolish the building in the 1930s and he was surprised to find that the walls were puddled – that is, willow branches woven together and filled out with mud. When Walter was young, he would go skating in the Fold during the winter, which was possible because the drainage was not good. If you could not afford skates the clogger down the road would make special irons to fit on your clogs.

Godley Hill Fold, 1910.

Harrison Fold, Newton, is reputed to be the birthplace of Tim Bobbin who was regarded as the first of a school of Lancashire dialect writers.

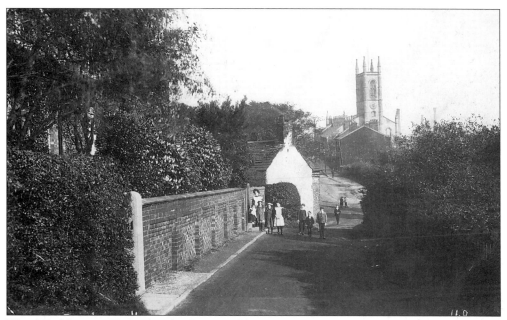

Wood End Lane in Hyde after the First World War.

The Thompson family outside their home on Werneth Low Road. Nancy, Ellen, and Henry are on the back row, and at the front, with the dog, James, are Sam and Joseph.

Mr and Mrs William Cooper at home on the Newton Hurst estate. They lived in one of the 22 houses built by Jackson & Welch, owners of Newton Mill, the manufacturers of stationery. Mr Cooper was an engineer at the mill.

A view of a kitchen in Bottom Street, Newton, showing spoiled bread in the oven. This was due to a great flood in the area experienced in May 1906.

This was the terminus for the trams from Ashton and Stockport. No doubt the Grapes Hotel provided a very good and welcome stopping place.

Werneth Lodge and the surrounding grounds were given to the town by Mrs Aspland and her son on 11 August 1919. Originally, in 1922, the grounds were opened as a public park. The house itself was converted into a maternity hospital. It was known as the Arthur Palmer Aspland Maternity Home and it was formally opened on 1 October 1931 by Mrs Aspland.

Hyde Hospital on Backbower Lane was opened on 17 June 1905.

Greenfield Street School was opened on 12 December 1929 by Councillor (Revd) J.S. Burgess, Chairman of the Education Committee.

Holy Trinity Church, Gee Cross, in 1907. The land for a church and school combined was donated by Mr Tatton of Wythenshawe in 1858. Later he provided more land and a building fund for a separate church, which was completed in 1873. Previously, the Church of England congregation had been forced to travel to St Paul's in Compstall.

The first place of worship for Church of England attenders was here at St George's Church in Hyde. It was erected on 28 May 1831, which was a Whit Saturday. Four years later a grand bazaar was organized to raise money for a school. It received the patronage of Her Majesty Queen Adelaide, consort of William IV. The Queen gave nine specimens of her own needlework, which raised over £100 towards the funds.

The public baths on Union Street were opened on 4 May 1889 as a memorial of Queen Victoria's Golden Jubilee. They were enlarged in 1913. During the Second World War they were converted into a British restaurant. The building to the right is the library and technical school, which was opened on 18 February 1899.

Hyde cemetery, opened in 1894.

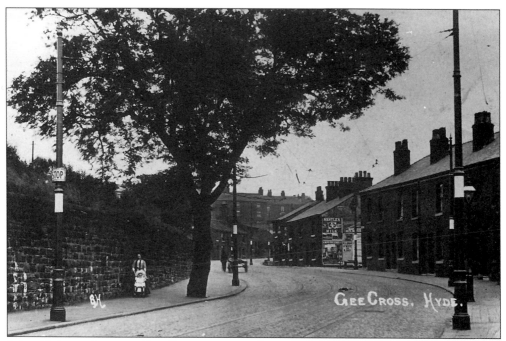

It is said that to be a true Gee Cross person one has to be born the other side of the 'Big Tree'. To the left of the tree is the Diamond reservoir, which has now been converted into a playing field with a memorial dedicated to those who fell in service in Ireland and the Falklands.

The 'Big Tree' had been a landmark for over 100 years and was a most welcome sight in the days when the present road to Stockport was a lonely country lane. There was strong resentment when, because it was a hazard to double-decker buses, the tree had to be cut down in 1934.

These are the gates and lodge of Kingston House on Manchester Road, Hyde. The Sidebottoms, who owned Kingston Mill, resided here. They were the first family to erect mills in the area, initially using water power, later steam, and they were one of the sponsors of the Peak Forest Canal.

The drawing room at Kingston House.

The beautiful Adam fireplace in the drawing room.

Pole Bank, Gee Cross. This beautifully styled Georgian house was built in the early nineteenth century by Thomas Ashton. It is a two-storey building with a double deep central staircase, and the front elevation has a classical porch with Ionic pillars. The Ashton family had farmed in the area since the sixteenth century, and eventually became cotton mill owners of great esteem.

Muslin Street, Newton, in the 1930s, when there was little traffic about and children were able to play games in the middle of the road.

Bay windows in Talbot Road, formerly Muslin Street.

The houses on the left of Joel Lane were known as 'Fender Row', due to the fact that one had to step down from the pathway to the houses. The church opposite was the Primitive Methodist Church.

Diamond Row Cottages in Gee Cross were situated between the wall of the reservoir and Stockport Road. The demolition enabled the width of the road at this point to be almost doubled.

Newton Cottages, 1912, built by J. & J. Ashton for their employees.

Sundial Cottage stood in Pudding Lane, Godley, from 1697 to 1980. A sundial was attached to the front of the house, hence its name.

Newton Lodge in Hyde Park.

Kensington House, Gee Cross, was the home of the Robinson family for many years. The builder Samuel Robinson, who built Hyde Town Hall, lived here with his wife, Elizabeth.

Abbotsford, Godley Green, was at one time the abode of Mr Fred Highham, editor of the *Cheshire Post* and, previous to that, editor and manager of the *North Cheshire Herald*. In 1907 he wrote and published *Biographical Sketches of the Middleton Family*.

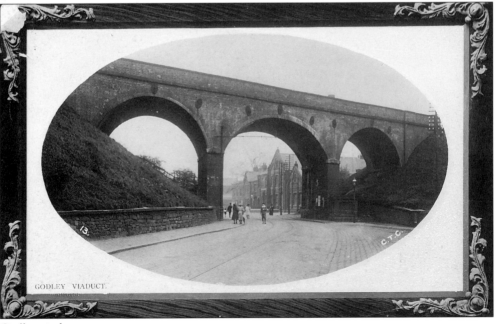

Godley viaduct.

The post office on the corner of Schofield Street, Newton.

George Street was the longest street in Hyde until 1970, when it disappeared to make way for the motorway.

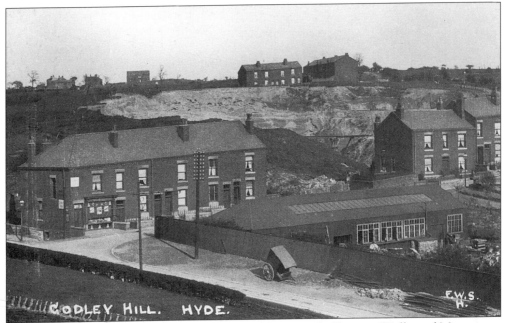

The factory on the right at Godley Hill was in turn Mansteads, Planters, Walls, and Mattersons. In the background you can see the sand pits of Godley.

Swindels Fold, Godley, *c.* 1910, generally known as A.B.C. Lane. The name came about due to the fact that the land on either side of the lane was split up into allotments, each one being given a letter of the alphabet for identification.

Stockport Road, Gee Cross, showing the Grapes Hotel on the left and the Boy and Barrel on the right. Many were the times in the past when these two establishments offered entertainment in the form of bull-baiting and cock-fighting. After baiting, the bull would be killed and sold off cheaply to the poorer people.

Demolition of the Boy and Barrel in the 1930s, carried out by the local building firm Armitages.

Originally, Godley Hall Inn was a farmstead and only became an inn after the owner of a pub on Godley Hill decided to give up the licence. The date inscribed over the door is 1718.

Bank Top, Hyde. The building with the shutters is Bank Top Inn.

Sunday dinner time at the Travellers Call, Joel Lane, 1930s. To the right of the pub are the old planking sheds where felt hats were made. The work was hot and steamy, so when work was finished the pub was very conveniently placed. Eventually the establishment was closed due to complaints from local residents.

George Hotel, Norbury Street, Hyde, in the 1930s.

Hyde Town Hall, built by Samuel Robinson in 1885.

This picture postcard of Thornley Fold at St George's Parsonage and Wood End Lane was posted to New Zealand in 1905 and eventually found its way back to England. The lane leads down to Captain Clarke's bridge which spans the Peak Forest Canal.

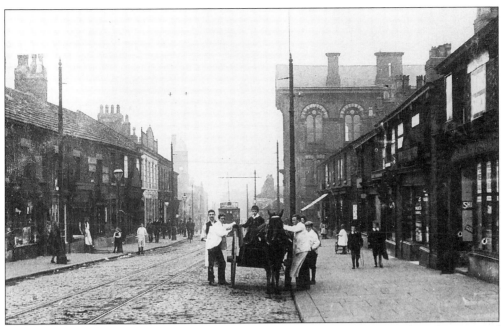

The large building on the right is the Mechanics Institute, which was situated on the corner of Market Street and Union Street.

A typical Victorian scene in 1904, with the blue No. 14 tram from Ashton entering Market Street *en route* to Gee Cross. It was at this point that the original ten houses of Red Pump Street stood. To the right is Pipers Penny Bazaar, and on the left is the chemist's shop.

The tram terminus at Mottram Road, Godley.

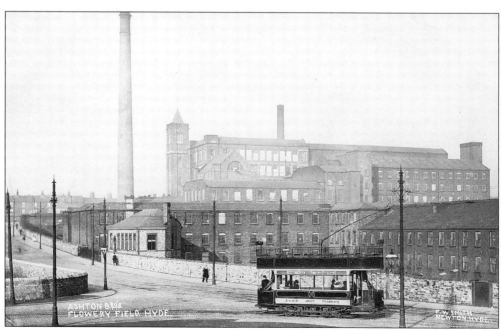

The textile firm of Ashton Brothers' mill complex: Carrfield Mill, Bayleyfield Mill, and Balaclava Mill.

*Three*
# Trade

This clock tower once stood at the corner of Apethorn Lane and Stockport Road, Gee Cross. It was built by the Ashtons to ensure that their employees would get to work on time. There was an inscription around the clock face which read 'Whilst thou lookest I fly'.

Ladies walking down Newton Street in Hyde on their way to work at Ashton Brothers in the early 1900s.

Although Ashton Brothers operated several mills around Hyde, the bulk of the firm's great productive energies were focussed on the complex of factory buildings at Carrfield. The nucleus of these was the Hollow Factory, better known as Carrfield Mill, which was constructed about 1810 by Samuel and Thomas Ashton. This photograph was taken in September 1921 and shows the variety of transport the firm used.

Throstle Bank Mill was another Ashton Brothers establishment, built in 1869. Cloth production began here in 1871. The factory, built alongside the Peak Forest Canal and adjacent to Hyde Junction and Romily railway, is a reminder of how much a firm like Ashtons depended on good transport links to bring in raw materials and dispatch finished products.

The weaving shed at Ashton Brothers.

A sizing machine at the firm in 1921. This was the last process applied to the thread before it was passed on to the weaving frames. It prevented the growth of mildew and strengthened the thread, giving a better weave.

Busy day in Hyde in 1905 when Greenfield Mill was still in operation and stood proudly next to the Town Hall. It was once a five-storey building but was later reduced to three storeys. The first part of the mill was built by 'Sally Rhodes' and consequently it was known as 'Sally Rhodes' Factory'. Originally, it was powered by horse and gin but when steam was introduced John Howard enlarged the premises. Production stopped in 1911 and prior to demolition in 1916 it was used by the Volunteer Services, who were drilled here, and trained for the First World War. It was a Thursday, 19 March, when the steeplejack began the demolition of the chimney, which had been a landmark in the centre of the town for over 100 years.

Slack Mill, at the centre of the picture, stood at the junction of Stockport Road and Hyde Lane. It was founded by Joseph Horsefield in 1809, when Stone Mill on Richmond Hill, Gee Cross, in which he had begun his cotton manufacturing career, became too small for his expanding business.

Workers from Slack Mill, Hyde, *c.* 1910. On the far right, bottom row, is Mr Rowbotham.

Directors of Slack Mill in the early 1900s.

GEE CROSS 568

A vista of chimneys seen from Lord Derby Road, Gee Cross. The chimney in the foreground is part of the old bone mill of Gee Cross in near proximity to Hyde Chapel. The area in front is Wych Fold Farm.

Howard Whittaker of Silver Hill, Gee Cross, was known as the 'King of Hyde' by his generation. He owned the stone quarry at Hunt Croft, which was also known as Whittakers Whim. It was a five-storey building built beneath the high road opposite Treacle Hill. He envisaged having a market place here, but the scheme did not come to fruition. In later years, beautiful gardens were constructed around the pond, which was frequented in turn by swimmers, skaters, and swans.

Gee Cross Mill was built by the banks of the Peak Forest Canal, which gave access to the local railway and the main roads to Manchester, Ashton, and Stockport. Only the iron gates still remain, and are used as the entrance to modern housing.

Gibraltar Mill, which gained its power from the River Tame.

The thirty-nine steps leading down
to the site of Gibraltar Mill.

Auto-Masters in the 1980s, a small business that started in a small shed in Denton and eventually developed into a large modern engineering works. To the left is Hyde Gas Works, which was discontinued in 1988.

Auto-Masters before modernisation, showing the old warehouses along the canal leading to Ashton.

Cotton mule spinning at J.H. Radcliffe & Sons in 1924. Mr Harry Driver is on the left.

Construction of the Queen Adelaide reservoir in Gee Cross, now the site of the village green.

Hyde Telephone Exchange in Onward Street in the 1950s, with the supervisors and operators, before it closed in 1958 and went automatic.

Mr Norman Adshead of Holmes and Adshead, the high-class ladies' and gentlemen's tailors in Corporation Street. The photograph was taken in 1941 for use on an identity card with endorsement for the Special Constabulary during the Second World War.

The last horse to be shod at Smithy Fold by the uncle of Margaret Walker (*née* Hyde).

Mr Edward Lewis, a railway guard (left), photographed with the Station Master and a co-worker at Godley Station.

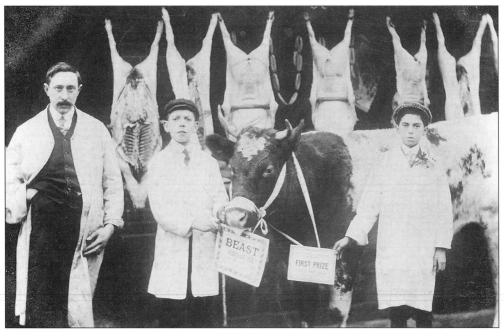

Fred Holt with his assistants and his prize-winning bull.

Holts had a butcher's shop in Market Street, and alongside his meat in the shop window he displayed his prize certificates. He was noted for his prompt deliveries.

On the site of the old Hippodrome in Clarendon Street was Hetts sweet shop. In the 1960s, the theatre was altered to become a supermarket, which was opened by Morecambe and Wise, along with Freddie Frinton.

The corner off-licence on Croft Street.

No. 7 Clarendon Place, Hyde, in 1882, with 'Happy Holland' and Mr Andrew.

Hyde Equitable Co-op Society was formed in 1862, and their new premises, which produced and sold goods for every occasion, were opened in 1929.

Christmas at the Co-op.

Everything for the man about town.

Mr W. Broadbent, who dressed this window for a competition, was the manager of Arnolds up to 1939, the proprietor being Mr J. Mossop. The shop was in the Borough Arcade off Clarendon Street.

*Four*
# Social and Leisure

The Godley Hill men were noted over a wide area for their morris dancing. They visited Knutsford, Blackpool, Buxton, Bolton, Southport, Garstang and Manchester, along with many other venues. They did regular shows at Belle Vue, Ashton, Mottram, and Hyde. They eventually became known as the Godley Hill Royal Dancers after one of the troop who was married on the same day as King Edward VII. The group ended its activities at the commencement of the First World War in 1914, but it was revived in 1931 for the Jubilee celebrations.

The Back Lane Club.

*Ali Baba and the Forty Thieves* performed at Talbot Road Methodist Church in Newton, around 1933.

In the early 1900s St George's School acted out *Maritina* to the delight of parents and relatives.

In March 1931, Hyde Lads' Club had a fancy dress ball and the winners were: back row (left to right) Olwen Johnson, Dorothy Wild, Peggy Wild, Therma Paterson, Phyllis Robinson, Alisa Ellison, Gladys Hodgson, Marion Lingard. Centre: Ruth Woodhall, Freda Lawler, May Bardsley. Seated: James Bourne, Elizabeth Danby, and Kenneth Higham.

Percy Davis (right) as one of the ugly sisters in *Cinderella* on stage in the church hall at St Mary's Church, Newton, in 1949.

The cast of the pantomime *Babes in the Wood* at St Mary's Church in 1948. Marjorie Davis and her sister Maureen were the babes.

In October 1934, Hyde Cine Society made a film called *Targets of Fate*. Here they are shooting one of the outside scenes at Bowlacre Lane, Gee Cross.

A fancy dress ball at Hyde Town Hall in 1932. This photograph shows only half the contestants, with the Mayor and Mayoress on the left. On the bottom row, second from right, is Kathleen Adams (*née* Adshead) dressed as the famous golliwog of the Robertson's jam logo.

St Thomas's Church Lads' Brigade Cadets in 1916.

Zion Congregational Church Boys' Life Brigade. The group was formed in 1909 only to be disbanded about 1915 owing to the First World War. The boys gained sound training in discipline and the moulding of character. More than twenty of these young men made the supreme sacrifice.

Zion Congregational Band.

Werneth Golf Club House.

Greenfield Street School won the Schoolboys' Shield in 1933. They defeated Flowery Field School in the finals of the Schools Knock-out Competition. On the left is Greenfield Street, on the right, Flowery Fields.

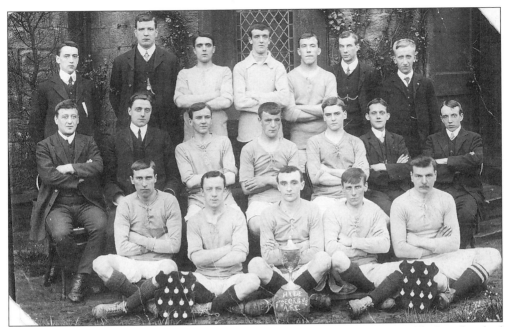

St George's Amateur Football Club in the early 1900s, displaying the cup and badges they had won.

St George's Football Club in 1910, with Fred Robinson second to the right on the front row.

Gee Cross Gymnastic Team stand proudly with their trophies.

Hyde Ladies' Hockey Club in 1933, after winning the Senior Flags and cup in the 5th Division of the North West Hockey League. Back row: (left to right) E. Gregory, B. Hibbert, M. Grimshaw, M. Bann, D. Newman, D. Parkin, M. Tetlow. Second row from the back: V. Dearden, M.W. Robinson, W. Bolland, M. Torkington, E. Hall, M.E. Cross, M. Marsden, H. Firth. Third row from the back: L. Warren, M. Mather, S.H. Wilde, E. Sheard, F. McCallum, E. Wells, E.M. Grimshaw, H. Hancock. Front row: D Pickup, I. Baddeley, M.B. Adamson, B. Roberts, D. Lyon.

Hyde Seal Swimming Club, 1925. On the back row, first from the left, is Ivy Newton.

Pupils of Hyde's Elementary Schools in 1934, who won championships in the first amateur swimming gala of the Cheshire Elementary Schools' Association at Chester Baths. Back row: (left to right) P. Alcock (Flowery Field), F. Cook (St George's), M. Harrison (Flowery Field), B. Beswick (St Mary's), M. Green, M. Cooke, H. Parker (Leigh Street), F. Chadwick (Flowery Field), J. Newcombe (St George's). Middle row: J. Morris (St George's), C. Oldham (Leigh Street), J. Leigh and E. Jackson (Flowery Field), H. Knight (St George's), T. Walker (Leigh Street). Front row: S. Palmer (Holy Trinity), W. Brunt (Flowery Field), M. Pugh (Flowery Field), E. Palmer (Holy Trinity), M. Harper (St George's), and T. Bromley (Leigh Street).

A men's-only outing in the 1920s. Fourth from the front is Samuel Robinson, in his bowler hat.

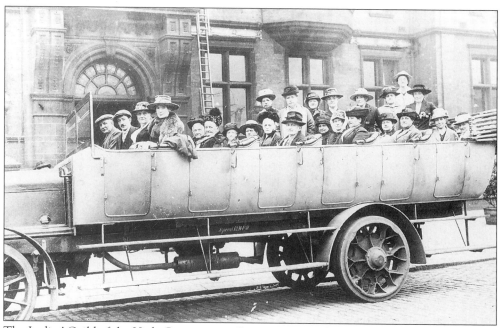

The Ladies' Guild of the Hyde Co-operative Society starting their outing from the Town Hall.

A coach trip, *c.* 1910, from the Irish Club on Ridling Lane.

Possibly a family day out to Blackpool.

In June 1883 St George's Rowing Club was inaugurated after much liaison with M.S. and L. Railways, who were the owners of the Peak Forest Canal. The first boathouse was erected in a field at Throstle Bank. Trips were made to Romily, Marple, and Daisy Nook. In addition to the pleasure outings some serious spells of rowing were indulged in. The club was re-organised in 1903 by Thomas Middleton, and on 10 December 1905 they were able to purchase another boat for the princely sum of £2 10s. A farm building at Wood End became their headquarters.

Hyde Ladies' Hockey Team after a match with Broadbottom Team (on the right).

*Five*
# Celebrations

Whit Friday 1919, outside St George's Church.

Whit Walks.

St Andrew's Church, John Street, Hyde, getting ready to start off their Procession of Witness during Whit Week.

Celebrations for the coronation of King Edward VII in 1902 on Market Street.

Whit Walks. The church congregation of Gee Cross is walking up the Gerrards, passing the Lamb Inn, in the early 1900s.

Joan and Kathleen, Whitsuntide, 1925.

George Street Methodists walking along Market Street with Sandra Whittaker on the right clutching her basket of flowers in her left hand and holding the banner ribbon in her right.

The gathering of the Newton Churches on Whit Friday 1964 for a communal hymn-singing in the 'George and Dragon Square', along with the Mayor, Mr Cullen, the Mayoress, and their son.

Hyde Baptist Church, 1966.

Godley Hill decorated for the coronation of King Edward VII.

At all-important celebrations there was the roasting of an ox, to be served to the people of Hyde.

A children's tea party in 1931 for the Jubilee.

Hyde Town Hall being decked out in her finery at the end of the First World War.

Even inside the weaving shed at Ashton Brothers flags and buntings were displayed at the end of the war.

The 57 member states of the League of Nations were represented by St George's scholars, each carrying a flag of the nation they represented, 1933.

A score of children from Hyde Baptist School made this tableau, 'Let Britannia Lead the Peace Crusade', in 1933.

The local men of Hatteresley posed in the Chapman's Arms fields to celebrate peace in 1918.

A gathering of the children of Hattersley for the peace celebrations.

The ladies of Hattersley in their finery, celebrating peace.

Sam Driver's coming-of-age party held at 6.00pm at the Town Hall on Saturday 9 August 1930.

Hilda Brian's twenty-first birthday party, held at the P.S.A. Hall in 1923. It was in 1993 that on the discovery of this photograph Hilda, then 91 years old, identified most of the people in the photograph. They are, back row: Sally Jones, Polly Much, Mabel Jefferies, Harold Beamont, -?-, Vera Orpet, -?-, -?-, Susie Carter, -?-, Archie Brome. Next to back row: Reg Brome, Jack Ingle, Annie Gregory, Austin Gregory, Edith Mansfield, -?-, -?-, Wilfred Stafford, Alice Bowden, Ann Leigh, -?-, Gladys Knowly, George Knowly. Next row: Doris Brian, Liza Hill, Ginny Sowter, Mary Murray, -?-, Janet Wilde, May ?, Fred Leigh, Mr and Mrs Ashworth, -?-, Connie Wyche, Beatrice Broome, Ida Mortou, Annie Broome. Front row: Mrs Lowe, George Orpet, Clare Orpet, Horace Orpet, Hilda Brian, Mary Anne Brian, Fred Brian, Beatrice Lowe, Harold Lowe, Annie Harrison, Jack Harrison. The two people sitting on the floor are Mr Shawcross and Furness Broome.

The May Queen of Leigh Street School.
Back row: Gerald Billinge, -?-, -?-, Arthur
Preece, -?-, -?-, John Chatterton. Front row:
Marjorie Platt, Jeam Mumford, Eric Stone,
Kathleen Lewis, Betty Bramall, Hilda
Birchall.

Left to right are: Muriel Smith, Barbara
Merrick (the May Queen), and Margaret
Bradley of Leigh Street Senior School.

Sadie Marsden, the May Queen of Flowery Field School.

In 1926, Dorothy Higingbottom was Leigh Street's May Queen.

The Band of Hope Queen in the 1930s.

Margaret Cooper (*née* Pimblett) in 1941,
as the May Queen at Flowery Field
Unitarian Church.

Zion Congregational Church in Peel Street in 1936 held the crowning of the Rose Queen in the Sunday School. The retiring Rose Queen was Phyllis Kempster.

Hyde Town Hall decorated for the celebration of the coronation of Queen Elizabeth II in 1953.

Children from St George's day school celebrating Empire Day in the 1920s.

Diamond Jubilee celebrations at Holy Trinity School, Gee Cross. Left to right: Mr J.E. Pickforn, Mr J. Bowker, Mr W. Widdowson, Mrs Wright, Mrs J. Shaw, Mr G. Cunliffe, Canon J.P. Richmond, Mrs Dimmock, Mrs Richmond and Mr G.B. Grocott. Seated is Mrs J. Bowker.

Each year in the month of August, Hyde held its Wakes Weeks. These were two weeks when most of the factories and shops closed down and the employees went on their annual holidays. Hyde always held a fair at this time, and it was situated opposite the Town Hall on the Market Square. This is the fair in 1950.

*Six*

# Institutions

The National Reserve Club.

The Gee Cross section of the Hyde Special Constabulary on duty during the Second World War. Back row, from the left, Mr Norman Adshead, Mr Nixon. Front row: -?-, Mr George Merrick (who owned the High Class Confectionery on Stockport Road, Gee Cross), -?-.

Hyde A.R.P. outside Bayley Hall, Hyde Park.

The 'New Connection' from George Street parading down Greenfield Street in the early 1930s.

The Boys' Brigade stands ready for inspection in St George's School yard.

These are the 'Manchester Pals Regiment'. Many of Hyde's young lads were in this group.

Mr Norman Adshead in his Royal Army Medical Corps uniform during the First World War.

Hyde Police Force in 1935, when the Chief Constable was William Smith.

Trinity National School, Gee Cross, 1905, when Mr Bowker, on the left, was the Headmaster. On the third row from the back, on the left, are -?-, Laura Weston and Annie Weston, and in the middle of the front row is Mary Ellen Weston. The school, which is in Higham Lane, was later known as Holy Trinity.

St George's School, when Mr Wood was the Headmaster. On the far right, second row, is Norman Adshead, who was born in 1895.

St George's in 1931, class 9. Mr Wood was still the headmaster. The class teacher was Miss Partridge. The third girl from the left on the second row is Kathleen Adams (*née* Adshead).

Miss Gibbons' class at St Mary's Church of England School, Newton, in the 1930s.

Schoolchildren from St Andrew's, George Street, Hyde.

Leigh Street School in the early 1900s.

Leigh Street School, Class 5, in 1931. The teacher on the left was Miss Babbage and the one on the right was Miss Beard. On the front row, second from right, is Alice Morris.

Leigh Street School, 1937. Back row, left to right: Miss Moores, Marjorie Hartley, John Morris, Peter Seller, Maurice Redfern, -?-, ? Gosling, Eric Heathcote, George Gregory, -?-. Middle row: Billy Goddard, -?-, Dennis Batty, Alfred Bridgehouse, Terence Chaplin, Paul Hargreaces, Gerald Chant, -?-, Robert Hamer, Fred Dodd. Front row: -?-, -?-, June Hirst, Margaret Barlow, Murrial Hibbert, Sheila Sharp, Doreen Ashworth, -?-, -?-.

Holy Trinity, Gee Cross, in 1918. Back row: (left to right) Ann Leigh, Margaret Oldham, Beatrice Emery, Liza Hill, Ginny Sowter, Mary ?, Doris Booth, Mary Inglefield. Next row: Baby Ada Bennett and her mother, Hilda Opet (née Brian), Mrs Ashworth, -?-, Beatrice Lowe (née Brian), Gertie Binyon, Annie Richardson, Lydia Bennett, Wilfred Bennett, Sam Penny, ? Whitehead Seated: Annie Wilson, May Hogg, Polly Hill, Annie Neild (née Wilson), Janet Wilde, May ? Ethel Ives, Annie Mansfield. Kneeling: Norman Bennett, Maggie Swindells, Alice Bowden (née Leigh), -?-, -?-, John Wilson, -?-, Florence Wilson (née Bennett). The group members were identified by Hilda Orpet.

Left: St George's Primary School, 1938. Back row: (left to right) -?-, -?-, Albert Sharples, Dean Wilde, -?-, -?-, -?-. Next row: -?-, -?-, Walter Binyon, Neville Robinson (with his drum), Beryl Fish, -?-, ? Ogden, -?-, Barry Lowe, -?-, Gordon Henshaw, -?-, -?-, Albert Tipper (on the triangle). Front row: Dorothy Harrison, Dorothy Hickling, ? Wibberly, Joyce Ashworth, -?-, Jean Broadbent, Denis Magee, and Marjorie Lowe.

*Seven*

# People of Hyde

Joshua Bradley sitting in his carriage outside the Commercial Inn, Birch Lane, Ashton Road, in the latter part of the nineteenth century. He started work as a 'little piecer' at Newton Mills and in the course of time progressed to management. He was born in Further Lane, Hattersley, on 8 April 1817, and died on 16 November 1898. During his lifetime he encouraged people to become educated. He donated to Hyde the clock and bells for the Town Hall.

Joseph Mycock held a seat on the local governing body of Hyde for 54 years. He was associated with Hyde Lane Sunday School, Union Street Chapel, and went on from there to help found the Zion Chapel in Gee Cross. Here, he acted as superintendent for forty years. He was the First Magistrate of the Borough in 1893, performing many other public services, including a term of office as Mayor in 1887/8.

John Thornley was Hyde Chapel's warden from 1879-1844, and Honorary Secretary 1885-1903. he was Chairman of Hyde Local Board and one of the First Aldermen of Hyde. For a number of years he was manager at Ashton Brothers mills.

Frances Lockett, aged 21, was voted Hyde's first Cotton Queen and later named Britain's Cotton Queen. She stepped from obscurity as a weaver at Newton Mill to national fame in a few weeks. At her civic reception 20,000 people welcomed her. She rode through the decorated streets in an open landau drawn by four bay horses. Mounted police led the procession followed by the Kingston Mill Band, Mrs Hamilton's troupe of Morris Dancers, 300 employees of J & J Ashton Ltd (Newton Mill), members of Hyde Lads' Club, forty motor cars, and Hyde Borough Band.

The marriage of Phillip Charles Potts to Edith Cheetham, *c*. 1905.

Charles Potts, 1890.

Graham Potts in 1943, later to be a well-known dentist in Hyde.

The Mayor, Mr Cullen, and his wife, the Mayoress, and their son. The headline in the local paper read: 'Son Sparks Off a Chain Reaction'.

Mr and Mrs James Adshead, who were married on 29 January 1872. The photograph was taken by a Mrs Sam Radcliffe of Newton Street.

Mr and Mrs James Adshead and their family, who lived at Wood End Lane, in 1906. The young boy kneeling is Norman Adshead, Kathleen Adams' father.

Mr J.V.A. Danby, the first Chief Constable of Hyde, in 1898. He held the office for 33 years, and in that time he developed an exemplary force and Hyde became noted for having such a small number of crimes. In 1911 he received the Coronation Long Service Medal and at Buckingham Palace in 1928 he was presented with the Police Medal by the King for exemplary service. Along with his responsible job he found time to be concerned with the social activities and welfare of the town. He was the founder of the Hyde Lads' Club.

The funeral of J.V.A. Danby on 27 December 1931. He was buried at Hyde Cemetery.

Arthur Phillip Adams served with the Merchant Navy as a radio officer from 1940 to 1945. He married Kathleen Adshead on 22 September 1956.

A visit from the Duke of Gloucester to open Hyde Lads' Club in Beeley Street. Thomas Middleton, the Mayor, is standing next to the Duke, and then the Mayoress and their daughter.

Tom Blower, Malinda Cullen, and Harry Cullen.

Kathleen Adams, who was in the
WRNS from 1943 to 1946. The
photograph was taken in the
Portsmouth area approaching D-
day.

Bill Cullen's relatives 140 years ago. They lived in Woodend Lane. Back row: (left to right) Edith, Mrs Cullen, Helen, Bertha, Mr Cullen, and Sam. In front are Dick, Laura, Jim, Kate, and Mandy.

Revd Mr Dawson, the vicar of St George's Church, on 11 August 1936.

Mrs Emily Shaw, who worked as housekeeper for Revd Dawson.

The funeral of Ivy Wood, attended by her classmates, in 1919.

Private Norman Adshead on leave with his future wife, Miss Ida J. Cooper, who lived with their family in Meadow Avenue, August 1917.

Mr Oswald Adshead, Norman's brother, was in the 11th Battalion of the Cheshire Regiment. He fought in the Battle of Loos and was killed on 18 October 1915, aged 25, after only three weeks in the trenches. He was a well-known member of St George's Church, where he was a chorister, and when dances were held in the church he would act as M.C.

Arthur Robinson, Leonard Hopwood,
Dorothy Hopwood, and Ann Robinson.
In front is Judith Robinson and the baby
in the pram is Eileen Hopwood, all
playmates in Knott Fold.

George Gregory and Jack Morris getting down to
some serious cricket in Thomas Street.

In 1815, twin boys were born to Mrs Smith who lived in Rock Street, Gee Cross. They were named Robin and Jam. All their life they went everywhere together. When they walked down the street one would walk behind the other treading in the footsteaps of the first. They both dressed alike no-one was sure which was which. After their brother and sisters left home and their parents died, they went to live in a cellar under the end house in Stone Row on Mottram Old Road. Then they were known locally as 'the Cellar People'. Jam died in 1889 and his brother in 1890.

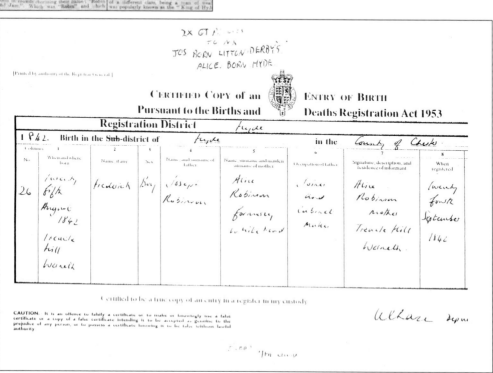

The Birth Certificate of Frederick Robinson, born in 1842, the seventh child in the family.

# HYDE ST GEORGE'S YOUNG MEN'S CLASS

## ROLL OF HONOUR AND MEMORIAL

J.E.TOLSON.    F.OLDFIELD.

W. BIRTWISTLE + J. LEIGH . +    J. WILSON + G.W. OLDHAM .

| | | | |
|---|---|---|---|
| D. ADAMS . | D. BOWLER . | F. BEARD . | R. BREERTON . |
| J. ARMITAGE . | L. BROWN . | W. BARNES . | H. BREERTON . |
| H. AINSWORTH . | F. BETHELL . | W. C. BARNES . | J. BOOTH . |
| N. ADSHEAD . | W. BURGESS . | W. BRADLEY . | A. BARDSLEY . |
| F. T. ARRANDALE . | D. B. BAILEY . | T. BOWLER . | A . BIRCHALL . |
| C. H. BANCROFT . | W. BAILEY . | F. BARDSLEY . | J. BURGESS . |
| J. BANCROFT . | W. BUTLER . | J. BARNETT . | F. BATTY . |
| W. BOWLER . | C. BEAMOND . | J.W. BATTY . | C. BRADWELL . |

| | | | |
|---|---|---|---|
| H. BOWDEN . | J. CARR . | W. FOX . | J. GREEN . M.M |
| W. BLACKHURST . | J. DANIELS . | W. M. FLETCHER . | A. GARLAND . |
| G. CUTTIFORD . | J. DOWNS . | T. FLETCHER . | J. GEE . |
| H. COOKE . | T. DOWNS . | R. FIRTH . | W. HALL . |
| J. COOPER . | N. DUCKWORTH . | E. FIRTH . | A. HIGGINBOTHAM . |
| T. CAMERON . | F. EASTWOOD . | F. FIRTH . | E. HALTON . |
| F. CLARKE . | A. ELLIS . | H. GUNNELL . | D. HAMPSON . |
| E. CROWLEY . | Alf. ELLIS . | M. K. GODLEY . | H. HORROCKS . |

| | | | |
|---|---|---|---|
| H.ᴿᴸᴰ HORROCKS . | J. HAUGHTON . | J. LEIGH . M.M. | W. MURRAY . |
| W. E. HALL . | F. HARTLEY . | Jᵒˢ. LANCASHIRE . | J. MORRIS . |
| H. HEROD . | C. INGHAM . | Jⁿᵗ. LANCASHIRE . | J. MELLOR . |
| W. HITCHEN . | J. JOHNSON . | J. LAWTON . | G. MYLES . |
| S. HOPKINSON . | J. JONES . | A. LOWE . | Hᵗ. MIDDLETON . |
| H. HARRISON . | W. JONES . | G. LEECH . | Hᵖ. MIDDLETON . |
| W. E. HEGINBOTHAM . | A. KEIGHLEY . | H. LINNEY . | H. NORGROVE . |
| W. HEWITT . | A. LEIGH . | W. LORD . | F. NORGROVE . |

| | | | |
|---|---|---|---|
| W. ORFORD . | H. PLANT . | E. REDFERN . | W. ROBINSON . |
| H. ORFORD . | F. PLANT . | S. REDFERN . | J. SAMUELS . |
| E. ORFORD . | F. PICKLES . | H. REDFERN . | E. SHAW . |
| J. OLDFIELD . | J.W. PARKER . | J. RIDGWAY . | A. G. SHAW . |
| H. OGDEN . | S. PARR . | A. RIGGS . | W. SHEPLEY . |
| A. OLDHAM . | C. J. PETERS . | N. ROWBOTTOM . | R. SAMUELS . |
| G. W. OAKES . | A. S. PLATT . | W. ROTHWELL . | A. SMITH . |
| W. PLANT . | J. POWELL . | J. ROBERTS . | A. STAINTHORPE . |
| | J. QUINN . | J. ROFF . | |

| | | | |
|---|---|---|---|
| W. SPENCER . | H. A. TAYLOR . M.M | A. WHITEHEAD . | Jᵗ. WILDE . |
| H. SPENCER . | Aᵗ. TAYLOR . | J. WHITEHEAD . | Hᵖ. WILDE . |
| G. C. SPENCER . | L. THOMPSON . | F. WALKER . | A. WHITELEY . |
| H. SILVER . | J. TETLOW . | H. WARBURTON . | J . WHITELEY . |
| P. SEELEY . | G. WHITEHURST . | N. WARBURTON . | H. WILSON . |
| A. SHERWIN . | | | Jᵇ. WHITEHEAD . |
| A. STOPFORD . | | | A. WILSON . |
| W. SHAW . | | | A. WOODHALL . |
| W. SMITH . | | | F . WOODHALL . |
| J. TAYLOR . | | | W.WRIGHT . J. WILDE . |

WAR DECLARED Aug 4ᵗʰ 1914

PEACE DECLARED June 28ᵗʰ 1919

MAKE · THEM · TO · BE · NUMBERED · WITH · THY
SAINTS · IN · GLORY · EVERLASTING

This memorial tablet was situated on the rear wall of St George's Church. It was later removed and is believed to be in the custody of Tameside Management.

125

A memorial obelisk to St George's Rowing Club. The Club's members who lost their lives in the First World War were Private Thomas H. Metcalfe, Private W. Whitehead, Corporal Arthur Robinson, Private William Wilson, and H.W. Bancroft. The base of the obelisk was built of 45 stones, one contributed by each member of the Club.

The Rowing Club embarked on the erection of a new boat house, the members removing 20 tons of solid clay to clear the site. Here, Mr Nicholas Warburton, Honorary Secretary, is laying the foundation stone on 20 May 1922.

Thomas Carter Beeley was born in 1870 and was the son of Thomas Beeley, J.P., of Pole Bank, and one of the leading local manufacturers of boilers. He was the first Chairman of the Joint Tramways and Electricity Board. He was also a magistrate and Chairman of the Watch Committee. During his term as Mayor (1899-1902) he proclaimed the accession of Edward VII. He later became a parliamentary candidate for the Liberal Party but due to ill health he had to resign. He and his wife worked very hard for local charities and the Indian Famine Fund.

Miss B. Betts of Hyde. An active member and speaker for the Hyde Socialist Party, Miss Betts later became Lady Barbara Castle.

Two young boys enjoying judo lessons at Hyde Lads Club.

Mr D.J. Sole, one of the engineers and cameramen who put Granada on the air. He was the first T.V. cameraman to shoot and transmit aerial views from an aeroplane.

# Stock List

## (Titles are listed according to the pre-1974 county boundaries)

### BERKSHIRE

**Wantage**
*Irene Hancock*
ISBN 0-7524-0146 7

### CARDIGANSHIRE

**Aberaeron and Mid Ceredigion**
*William Howells*
ISBN 0-7524-0106-8

### CHESHIRE

**Ashton-under-Lyne and Mossley**
*Alice Lock*
ISBN 0-7524-0164-5

**Around Bebington**
*Pat O'Brien*
ISBN 0-7524-0121-1

**Crewe**
*Brian Edge*
ISBN 0-7524-0052-5

**Frodsham and Helsby**
*Frodsham and District Local History Group*
ISBN 0-7524-0161-0

**Macclesfield Silk**
*Moira Stevenson and Louanne Collins*
ISBN 0-7524-0315 X

**Marple**
*Steve Cliffe*
ISBN 0-7524-0316-8

**Runcorn**
*Bert Starkey*
ISBN 0-7524-0025-8

**Warrington**
*Janice Hayes*
ISBN 0-7524-0040-1

**West Kirby to Hoylake**
*Jim O'Neil*
ISBN 0-7524-0024-X

**Widnes**
*Anne Hall and the Widnes Historical Society*
ISBN 0-7524-0117-3

### CORNWALL

**Padstow**
*Malcolm McCarthy*
ISBN 0-7524-0033-9

**St Ives Bay**
*Jonathan Holmes*
ISBN 0-7524-0186-6

### COUNTY DURHAM

**Bishop Auckland**
*John Land*
ISBN 0-7524-0312-5

**Around Shildon**
*Vera Chapman*
ISBN 0-7524-0115-7

### CUMBERLAND

**Carlisle**
*Dennis Perriam*
ISBN 0-7524-0166-1

### DERBYSHIRE

**Around Alfreton**
*Alfreton and District Heritage Trust*
ISBN 0-7524-0041-X

**Barlborough, Clowne, Creswell and Whitwell**
*Les Yaw*
ISBN 0-7524-0031-2

**Around Bolsover**
*Bernard Haigh*
ISBN 0-7524-0021-5

**Around Derby**
*Alan Champion and Mark Edworthy*
ISBN 0-7524-0020-7

**Long Eaton**
*John Barker*
ISBN 0-7524-0110-6

**Ripley and Codnor**
*David Buxton*
ISBN 0-7524-0042-8

**Shirebrook**
*Geoff Sadler*
ISBN 0-7524-0028-2

**Shirebrook: A Second Selection**
*Geoff Sadler*
ISBN 0-7524-0317-6

## DEVON

**Brixham**
Ted Gosling and Lyn Marshall
ISBN 0-7524-0037-1

**Around Honiton**
*Les Berry and Gerald Gosling*
ISBN 0-7524-0175-0

**Around Newton Abbot**
*Les Berry and Gerald Gosling*
ISBN 0-7524-0027-4

**Around Ottery St Mary**
*Gerald Gosling and Peter Harris*
ISBN 0-7524-0030-4

**Around Sidmouth**
*Les Berry and Gerald Gosling*
ISBN 0-7524-0137-8

## DORSET

**Around Uplyme and Lyme Regis**
*Les Berry and Gerald Gosling*
ISBN 0-7524-0044-4

## ESSEX

**Braintree and Bocking**
*John and Sandra Adlam and Mark Charlton*
ISBN 0-7524-0129-7

**Ilford**
*Ian Dowling and Nick Harris*
ISBN 0-7524-0050-9

**Ilford: A Second Selection**
*Ian Dowling and Nick Harris*
ISBN 0-7524-0320-6

**Saffron Walden**
*Jean Gumbrell*
ISBN 0-7524-0176-9

## GLAMORGAN

**Around Bridgend**
*Simon Eckley*
ISBN 0-7524-0189-0

**Caerphilly**
*Simon Eckley*
ISBN 0-7524-0194-7

**Around Kenfig Hill and Pyle**
*Keith Morgan*
ISBN 0-7524-0314-1

**The County Borough of Merthyr Tydfil**
*Carolyn Jacob, Stephen Done and Simon Eckley*
ISBN 0-7524-0012-6

**Mountain Ash, Penrhiwceiber and Abercynon**
*Bernard Baldwin and Harry Rogers*
ISBN 0-7524-0114-9

**Pontypridd**
*Simon Eckley*
ISBN 0-7524-0017-7

**Rhondda**
*Simon Eckley and Emrys Jenkins*
ISBN 0-7524-0028-2

**Rhondda: A Second Selection**
*Simon Eckley and Emrys Jenkins*
ISBN 0-7524-0308-7

**Roath, Splott, and Adamsdown**
*Roath Local History Society*
ISBN 0-7524-0199-8

## GLOUCESTERSHIRE

**Barnwood, Hucclecote and Brockworth**
*Alan Sutton*
ISBN 0-7524-0000-2

**Forest to Severn**
*Humphrey Phelps*
ISBN 0-7524-0008-8

**Filton and the Flying Machine**
*Malcolm Hall*
ISBN 0-7524-0171-8

**Gloster Aircraft Company**
*Derek James*
ISBN 0-7524-0038-X

**The City of Gloucester**
*Jill Voyce*
ISBN 0-7524-0306-0

**Around Nailsworth and Minchinhampton from the Conway Collection**
*Howard Beard*
ISBN 0-7524-0048-7

**Around Newent**
*Tim Ward*
ISBN 0-7524-0003-7

**Stroud: Five Stroud Photographers**
*Howard Beard, Peter Harris and Wilf Merrett*
ISBN 0-7524-0305-2

## HAMPSHIRE

**Gosport**
*Ian Edelman*
ISBN 0-7524-0300-1

**Winchester from the Sollars Collection**
*John Brimfield*
ISBN 0-7524-0173-4

## HEREFORDSHIRE
**Ross-on-Wye**
*Tom Rigby and Alan Sutton*
ISBN 0-7524-0002-9

## HERTFORDSHIRE
**Buntingford**
*Philip Plumb*
ISBN 0-7524-0170-X

**Hampstead Garden Suburb**
*Mervyn Miller*
ISBN 0-7524-0319-2

**Hemel Hempstead**
*Eve Davis*
ISBN 0-7524-0167-X

**Letchworth**
*Mervyn Miller*
ISBN 0-7524-0318-4

**Welwyn Garden City**
*Angela Eserin*
ISBN 0-7524-0133-5

## KENT
**Hythe**
*Joy Melville and Angela Lewis-Johnson*
ISBN 0-7524-0169-6

**North Thanet Coast**
*Alan Kay*
ISBN 0-7524-0112-2

**Shorts Aircraft**
*Mike Hooks*
ISBN 0-7524-0193-9

## LANCASHIRE
**Lancaster and the Lune Valley**
*Robert Alston*
ISBN 0-7524-0015-0

**Morecambe Bay**
*Robert Alston*
ISBN 0-7524-0163-7

**Manchester**
*Peter Stewart*
ISBN 0-7524-0103-3

## LINCOLNSHIRE
**Louth**
*David Cuppleditch*
ISBN 0-7524-0172-6

**Stamford**
*David Gerard*
ISBN 0-7524-0309-5

## LONDON
(Greater London and Middlesex)
**Battersea and Clapham**
*Patrick Loobey*
ISBN 0-7524-0010-X

**Canning Town**
*Howard Bloch and Nick Harris*
ISBN 0-7524-0057-6

**Chiswick**
*Carolyn and Peter Hammond*
ISBN 0-7524-0001-0

**Forest Gate**
*Nick Harris and Dorcas Sanders*
ISBN 0-7524-0049-5

**Greenwich**
*Barbara Ludlow*
ISBN 0-7524-0045-2

**Highgate and Muswell Hill**
*Joan Schwitzer and Ken Gay*
ISBN 0-7524-0119-X

**Islington**
*Gavin Smith*
ISBN 0-7524-0140-8

**Lewisham**
*John Coulter and Barry Olley*
ISBN 0-7524-0059-2

**Leyton and Leytonstone**
*Keith Romig and Peter Lawrence*
ISBN 0-7524-0158-0

**Newham Dockland**
*Howard Bloch*
ISBN 0-7524-0107-6

**Norwood**
*Nicholas Reed*
ISBN 0-7524-0147-5

**Peckham and Nunhead**
*John D. Beasley*
ISBN 0-7524-0122-X

**Piccadilly Circus**
*David Oxford*
ISBN 0-7524-0196-3

**Stoke Newington**
*Gavin Smith*
ISBN 0-7524-0159-9

**Sydenham and Forest Hill**
*John Coulter and John Seaman*
ISBN 0-7524-0036-3

**Wandsworth**
*Patrick Loobey*
ISBN 0-7524-0026-6

**Wanstead and Woodford**
*Ian Dowling and Nick Harris*
ISBN 0-7524-0113-0

## MONMOUTHSHIRE

**Vanished Abergavenny**
*Frank Olding*
ISBN 0-7524-0034-7

**Abertillery, Aberbeeg and Llanhilleth**
*Abertillery and District Museum Society and Simon Eckley*
ISBN 0-7524-0134-3

**Blaina, Nantyglo and Brynmawr**
*Trevor Rowson*
ISBN 0-7524-0136-X

## NORFOLK

**North Norfolk**
*Cliff Richard Temple*
ISBN 0-7524-0149-1

## NOTTINGHAMSHIRE

**Nottingham 1897–1947**
*Douglas Whitworth*
ISBN 0-7524-0157-2

## OXFORDSHIRE

**Banbury**
*Tom Rigby*
ISBN 0-7524-0013-4

## PEMBROKESHIRE

**Saundersfoot and Tenby**
*Ken Daniels*
ISBN 0-7524-0192-0

## RADNORSHIRE

**Llandrindod Wells**
*Chris Wilson*
ISBN 0-7524-0191-2

## SHROPSHIRE

**Leominster**
*Eric Turton*
ISBN 0-7524-0307-9

**Ludlow**
*David Lloyd*
ISBN 0-7524-0155-6

**Oswestry**
*Bernard Mitchell*
ISBN 0-7524-0032-0

**North Telford: Wellington, Oakengates, and Surrounding Areas**
*John Powell and Michael A. Vanns*
ISBN 0-7524-0124-6

**South Telford: Ironbridge Gorge, Madeley, and Dawley**
*John Powell and Michael A. Vanns*
ISBN 0-7524-0125-4

## SOMERSET

**Bath**
*Paul De'Ath*
ISBN 0-7524-0127-0

**Around Yeovil**
*Robin Ansell and Marion Barnes*
ISBN 0-7524-0178-5

## STAFFORDSHIRE

**Cannock Chase**
*Sherry Belcher and Mary Mills*
ISBN 0-7524-0051-7

**Around Cheadle**
*George Short*
ISBN 0-7524-0022-3

**The Potteries**
*Ian Lawley*
ISBN 0-7524-0046-0

**East Staffordshire**
*Geoffrey Sowerby and Richard Farman*
ISBN 0-7524-0197-1

## SUFFOLK

**Lowestoft to Southwold**
*Humphrey Phelps*
ISBN 0-7524-0108-4

**Walberswick to Felixstowe**
*Humphrey Phelps*
ISBN 0-7524-0109-2

## SURREY

**Around Camberley**
*Ken Clarke*
ISBN 0-7524-0148-3

**Around Cranleigh**
*Michael Miller*
ISBN 0-7524-0143-2

**Epsom and Ewell**
*Richard Essen*
ISBN 0-7524-0111-4

**Farnham by the Wey**
*Jean Parratt*
ISBN 0-7524-0185-8

**Industrious Surrey: Historic Images of the County at Work**
*Chris Shepheard*
ISBN 0-7524-0009-6

**Reigate and Redhill**
*Mary G. Goss*
ISBN 0-7524-0179-3

**Richmond and Kew**
*Richard Essen*
ISBN 0-7524-0145-9

## SUSSEX

**Billingshurst**
*Wendy Lines*
ISBN 0-7524-0301-X

## WARWICKSHIRE

**Central Birmingham 1870–1920**
*Keith Turner*
ISBN 0-7524-0053-3

**Old Harborne**
*Roy Clarke*
ISBN 0-7524-0054-1

## WILTSHIRE

**Malmesbury**
*Dorothy Barnes*
ISBN 0-7524-0177-7

**Great Western Swindon**
*Tim Bryan*
ISBN 0-7524-0153-X

**Midland and South Western Junction Railway**
*Mike Barnsley and Brian Bridgeman*
ISBN 0-7524-0016-9

## WORCESTERSHIRE

**Around Malvern**
*Keith Smith*
ISBN 0-7524-0029-0

## YORKSHIRE
(EAST RIDING)

**Hornsea**
*G.L. Southwell*
ISBN 0-7524-0120-3

## YORKSHIRE
(NORTH RIDING)

**Northallerton**
*Vera Chapman*
ISBN 0-7524-055-X

**Scarborough in the 1970s and 1980s**
*Richard Percy*
ISBN 0-7524-0325-7

## YORKSHIRE
(WEST RIDING)

**Barnsley**
*Barnsley Archive Service*
ISBN 0-7524-0188-2

**Bingley**
*Bingley and District Local History Society*
ISBN 0-7524-0311-7

**Bradford**
*Gary Firth*
ISBN 0-7524-0313-3

**Castleford**
*Wakefield Metropolitan District Council*
ISBN 0-7524-0047-9

**Doncaster**
*Peter Tuffrey*
ISBN 0-7524-0162-9

**Harrogate**
*Malcolm Neesam*
ISBN 0-7524-0154-8

**Holme Valley**
*Peter and Iris Bullock*
ISBN 0-7524-0139-4

**Horsforth**
*Alan Cockroft and Matthew Young*
ISBN 0-7524-0130-0

**Knaresborough**
*Arnold Kellett*
ISBN 0-7524-0131-9

**Around Leeds**
*Matthew Young and Dorothy Payne*
ISBN 0-7524-0168-8

**Penistone**
*Matthew Young and David Hambleton*
ISBN 0-7524-0138-6

**Selby from the William Rawling Collection**
*Matthew Young*
ISBN 0-7524-0198-X

**Central Sheffield**
*Martin Olive*
ISBN 0-7524-0011-8

**Around Stocksbridge**
*Stocksbridge and District History Society*
ISBN 0-7524-0165-3

## TRANSPORT

**Filton and the Flying Machine**
*Malcolm Hall*
ISBN 0-7524-0171-8

**Gloster Aircraft Company**
*Derek James*
ISBN 0-7524-0038-X

**Great Western Swindon**
*Tim Bryan*
ISBN 0-7524-0153-X

**Midland and South Western Junction Railway**
*Mike Barnsley and Brian Bridgeman*
ISBN 0-7524-0016-9

**Shorts Aircraft**
*Mike Hooks*
ISBN 0-7524-0193-9

This stock list shows all titles available in the United Kingdom as at 30 September 1995.

# ORDER FORM

The books in this stock list are available from your local bookshop. Alternatively they are available by mail order at a totally inclusive price of £10.00 per copy.

For overseas orders please add the following postage supplement for each copy ordered:
> European Union £0.36 (this includes the Republic of Ireland)
> Royal Mail Zone 1 (for example, U.S.A. and Canada) £1.96
> Royal Mail Zone 2 (for example, Australia and New Zealand) £2.47

Please note that all of these supplements are actual Royal Mail charges with no profit element to the Chalford Publishing Company. Furthermore, as the Air Mail Printed Papers rate applies, we are restricted from enclosing any personal correspondence other than to indicate the senders name.

Payment can be made by cheque, Visa or Mastercard. Please indicate your method of payment on this order form.

If you are not entirely happy with your purchase you may return it within 30 days of receipt for a full refund.

Please send your order to:

> The Chalford Publishing Company,
> St Mary's Mill,
> Chalford,
> Stroud,
> Gloucestershire
> GL6 8NX

This order form should perforate away from the book. However, if you are reluctant to damage the book in any way we are quite happy to accept a photocopy order form or a letter containing the necessary information.

# PLEASE WRITE CLEARLY USING BLOCK CAPITALS

Name and address of the person ordering the books listed below:

_____

_____

_____ Post code _____

Please also supply your telephone number in case we have difficulty fully understanding your requirements.     Tel.: _____ - _____

Name and address of where the books are to be despatched to (if different from above):

_____

_____

_____ Post code _____

Please indicate here if you would like to receive future information on books published by the Chalford Publishing Company.

____ Yes, please put me on your mailing list     ____ No, please just send the books ordered below

| Title | ISBN | Quantity |
|---|---|---|
| ................................................... | 0-7524-_____-___ | _____ |
| ................................................... | 0-7524-_____-___ | _____ |
| ................................................... | 0-7524-_____-___ | _____ |
| ................................................... | 0-7524-_____-___ | _____ |
| ................................................... | 0-7524-_____-___ | _____ |
| | Total number of books | _____ |

**Cost of books delivered in UK** = Number of books ordered @ £10 each =£ _____

**Overseas postage supplement** (if relevant)                              =£ _____

**TOTAL PAYMENT**                                                          =£ _____

Method of Payment        ❑ Cheque     ❑ Visa     ❑ Mastercard     **VISA**
Please make cheques payable to *The Chalford Publishing Company*     MasterCard

Name of Card Holder     _____

Card Number ❑❑❑❑❑❑❑❑❑❑❑❑❑❑❑❑❑❑❑❑❑❑

Expiry date ❑❑ / ❑❑

I authorise payment of £_____ from the above card

Signed _____